CHEETAH

by CAROLINE ARNOLD
Photographs by RICHARD HEWETT

MORROW JUNIOR BOOKS • NEW YORK

PHOTO CREDITS: Permission to use the following photographs is gratefully acknowledged: Jay Golden, Wildlife Safari, pages 26, 29; Pete Vogel, Wildlife Safari, pages 32–33.

1 2 3 4 5 6 7 8 9 10

Library of Congress Cataloging-in-Publication Data. Arnold, Caroline. Cheetah / by Caroline Arnold ; photographs by Richard Hewett.   p.   cm. Summary: Describes the physical characteristics, habits, and life cycle of cheetahs living in the wild and in captivity at zoos. ISBN 0-688-08143-6. ISBN 0-688-08144-4 (lib. bdg.)   1. Cheetahs—Juvenile literature.   [1. Cheetahs.]   I. Hewett, Richard, ill.   II. Title. QL737.C23A75 1989 599.74'428—dc19 88-39940 CIP AC

ACKNOWLEDGMENTS

We are extremely grateful to the staff of Wildlife Safari in Winston, Oregon, for their generous help and for giving us the opportunity to get to know their cheetahs and photograph them. In particular we want to thank Laurie Marker, Director of Education and International Cheetah Studbook Keeper (pictured above), for her expert advice and her contagious enthusiasm for these fascinating animals. We also give special thanks to Kerry Pessin, Damara, and the children of the Waldorf School in Eugene, Oregon, for their cooperation with the photos, and to John Cooper for his cheerful assistance throughout the project. And, as always, we thank our editor, Andrea Curley, for her continued support.

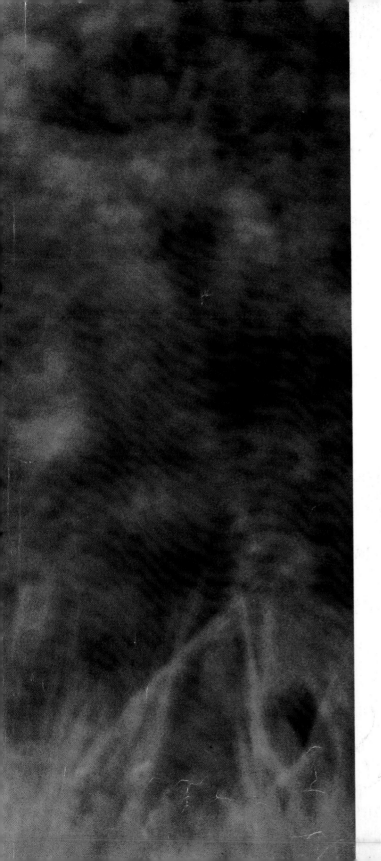

Sitting peacefully by her trainer's side, Damara gazes across the grassy hillside, her sleek body reflecting the warm afternoon sunshine. Damara's keen ears, like those of all cheetahs, are alert to every sound, and her sharp eyes can detect even the slightest movement. A combination of keen senses and powerful muscles make the cheetah one of the most skilled hunters of the African plain.

Damara is one of nine cheetahs that live at Wildlife Safari, an open-air animal park in southern Oregon. Unlike wild cheetahs, none of these animals will ever have to pursue wild game for a meal. Instead, a regular diet of fresh meat is provided for them by their keepers.

In the park, cheetahs, antelopes, and other animals roam freely across wooded grasslands. In many ways the land resembles the African savannah that is the cheetahs' natural home. The cheetah enclosure includes both open and wooded areas, rocks for climbing, a freshwater pond, and small shelters for rainy or cold weather. Except for not having to hunt for their food, the cheetahs live and behave much as they would in the wild. During the day visitors drive through the park and watch the animals through the windows of their vehicles.

Although cheetahs once lived in Africa, and in India and other parts of Asia, today they are found only in limited areas of eastern and southern Africa. With fewer than 15,000 animals left in the wild, this elegant large cat is one of the world's most endangered species. Hunting, disease, and the destruction of the cheetahs' natural home have all played a part in reducing the world population. Cheetahs have never been numerous, and without protection and special care, they are in serious danger of becoming extinct. By studying cheetahs, both in the wild and in captivity at zoos and animal parks, we can learn more about them. Then we will be better able to help them to survive in the future.

Wildlife Safari has one of the best programs for keeping and studying cheetahs in the world. Many of the cheetahs there have bred and produced young. Since the park opened in 1972, 97 baby cheetahs, called *cubs*, have been born. In the wild, cheetah cubs have less than a fifty percent chance of survival; but at places like Wildlife Safari, the absence of predators, plenty of food, and expert medical care give every cub a good chance to become an adult.

Most of the cheetah cubs born in the park have been raised by their mothers as they would be in the wild. However, when Damara was young she needed special medical care and had to be hand-raised by the keepers in the park nursery. Later she learned to obey commands and to interact with people.

Because Damara did not grow up with the other cheetahs, she is not used to living with them and they are not used to her. If Damara went into the main cheetah area, the other cheetahs would try to chase her away. Instead, Damara lives in her own en-closure near the main visitors' center of the park. Her trainer often takes her out on her leash so that visitors can get to know her better. It would be dangerous to go near a wild cheetah, but because Damara is tame, people can get close to her. Even so, her trainers are always careful to make sure she does not get frightened or annoyed.

Cheetahs are the easiest of the large cats to tame and have been associated with people for over 4,000 years. Pictures of cheetahs are found in ancient Egyptian tombs, and, for hundreds of years in India, maharajahs trained them to hunt. More recently, movie stars and royalty have kept them as pets.

Since the United States passed the Endangered Species Act in 1974, however, it has been against the law for private citizens to have cheetahs as pets. Today, only zoos and wildlife parks can keep cheetahs in captivity.

Most countries of the world have similar laws to protect wild animals in danger of extinction.

One day, a keeper came to Damara's enclosure and put the cheetah on her leash. Because Damara gets along so well with people, she often accompanies the park staff when they make visits to schools and community centers. Damara helps them to promote the cause of wildlife conservation and to educate people about cheetahs. Everyone who meets Damara is impressed both by her friendliness and her elegant beauty.

During the staff's talk Damara usually lies on a table where the audience can see her. She seems to enjoy being the center of attention and often purrs so loudly that people can hear her even in the back of the room. When the talk is finished, the audience is allowed to come close to Damara and pet her. Most people are surprised to discover that cheetah fur is not soft at all, but more like the texture of a coarse brush.

14

The first cheetahs probably evolved about 20 million years ago in Africa. About 3.8 to 1.9 million years ago, there was a giant cheetah about the size of a modern lion. Cheetahs like those alive today first appeared about 200,000 years ago. Their scientific name is *Acinonyx jubatus*.

Like lions, leopards, and the common house cat, cheetahs are members of the cat family, or felids. They share many characteristics with other cats, but they also have their own unique features. For instance, the shape of the cheetah is different from that of most other cats. The cheetah has a larger chest, leaner body, and longer legs. Also, unlike most other cats, the cheetah cannot fully retract its claws.

The name *cheetah* is derived from the Hindu word *chita*, which means "spotted one." The distinguishing marks of a cheetah are the long, tear-drop-shaped lines on each side of the nose.

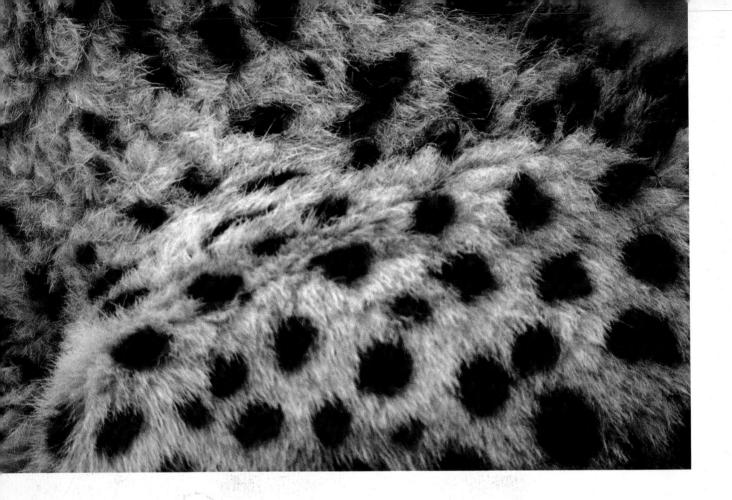

No two cheetahs have exactly the same pattern of spots, so these markings can be used to identify individual animals. Most of the keepers at Wildlife Safari can recognize individual cheetahs by their markings and their behavior, as well as by any unique feature they may have. Damara's special characteristic is an unusual kink in her tail.

Like that of other cheetahs, Damara's coat is light tan, or buff-colored, with black spots that measure from 1¼ to 2 inches (3.2 to 5.1 centimeters) across. In between these marks are smaller, less distinct spots. There are no spots on the belly, which is white, and on the tail the spots merge to form four to six dark rings. The tail ends in a bushy, white tuft.

Female (left), male (right).

While the cheetah's tan fur is short, the fur of the black spots is slightly longer and softer. Along the back of the neck, the fur forms a small ruff, or mane. Sometimes this mane is larger in males.

Although male cheetahs are often slightly bigger than females, it is difficult to tell males and females apart by appearance alone. An adult cheetah usually weighs between 100 and 140 pounds (45.4 and 63.6 kilograms) and stands about 30 inches (.76 meter) tall at the shoulder. The head and body are about 4 feet (1.2 meters) long, and the tail is usually half as long as the total body length.

Each morning at Wildlife Safari one of the keepers drives through the cheetah enclosure to check on the animals. The keeper locates each cheetah and takes note of any unusual behavior or if any animal appears to need medical care. If a cheetah does become sick, it is cared for by the park veterinarian.

Although the cheetahs in the park are used to people, most of them do not like to be handled, and hiss if a keeper gets too close. If they require medical treatments, the cheetahs are usually taken to the clinic, where they are anesthetized before being examined. Damara, on the other hand, has always been handled and does not appear to mind when her keepers need to perform routine examinations such as checking her ears or her paws.

The animal keepers also note if any of the cheetahs seems ready to mate. Unlike many other animals, cheetahs do not have a particular breeding season and can have young at any time of the year. At the park, if two cheetahs show interest in mating with each other, they are put together in an enclosure separate from the other cheetahs.

For one or two weeks before she is ready to mate, a female cheetah produces a special scent in her urine. This is a signal to males that she will be willing to mate soon. When a male cheetah first approaches her, the female allows him to sniff her. However, if he tries to get too close, the female will send him away with a swat of her paw. Only when she is ready to mate a week or so later will she let him come near.

The mating period lasts about a week, and when it is over, the male leaves. If the female becomes pregnant, she will give birth about fourteen weeks later. If she does not, the mating cycle will repeat itself in about ten days.

Female cheetahs typically breed about once every eighteen months and produce up to six cubs in a litter. At the park, pregnant females are put in separate enclosures so that they will not be disturbed by the other cheetahs when their cubs are born.

Shortly before she is ready to give birth, a female cheetah finds a quiet, hidden spot. This may be in the tall grass, under a low tree, in thick underbrush, or behind a clump of rocks. There, while she lies on her side, the tiny cubs are born. A newborn cub weighs about $7\frac{4}{5}$ to 10 ounces (222.9 to 285.7 grams) and is about 9 inches (.23 meter) long from the nose to the base of the tail.

Although cheetah cubs are blind and completely helpless at birth, they develop rapidly. At about five to ten days of age, their eyes open and they begin to crawl around the nest area. By the age of three weeks, the cubs can walk, and by six weeks they can follow their mother. A cheetah mother calls to her cubs by making low, birdlike, chirping sounds.

As in all mammals, a cheetah cub's first food is its mother's milk. The young cubs crowd together against their mother's belly, each searching for its own teat. The cubs gain weight steadily and at six weeks weigh about $5\frac{1}{2}$ pounds (2.5 kilograms). By five months of age, they weigh over 18 pounds (8.2 kilograms).

Unlike the fur of adult cheetahs, the fur of the newborn cubs is dark and the tiny spots are barely visible. Then, during the first few weeks of life, a thick coat, called a mantle, grows in, giving the cub a soft, furry appearance. Its dull, smoky-gray color helps the young cheetah to blend into the shadows, and so acts as a camouflage. The fur of the mantle is about 3 inches (7.7 centimeters) long. By making the tiny cub look larger than it really is, the mantle may help to protect it from some predators. In the wild, cheetah cubs are often killed by lions, hyenas, and other large animals. Between the ages of three and eight months, the mantle gradually falls out, revealing a coat underneath that is like that of an adult cheetah.

The young cubs' first teeth begin to appear at two weeks, and at four weeks they begin to eat meat. At first, their mother allows them to eat what she has killed. Later, when the cubs are about seven months old, they begin to hunt with their mother. Adult teeth come in when the cubs are ten to fourteen months old.

At about one year, cheetah cubs are learning to hunt by themselves, and by sixteen to eighteen months of age they are able to hunt independently. At about this time their mother is ready to mate again and leaves her cubs. Then they must survive on their own. Litter mates often remain together for a while after their mother leaves.

Young cheetahs reach full growth and can reproduce between sixteen and eighteen months of age. However, females usually do not produce young until they are two years old.

Like other cats, cheetahs are carnivores, or meat-eaters. Wild cheetahs eat a variety of small and medium-size animals, ranging from birds and rabbits to ostriches and antelopes. The most common meal of the cheetah in East Africa is a small antelope called Thompson's gazelle.

Although a cheetah rarely climbs tall trees, it will often jump onto a low branch or a rock to get a better view of the plain when searching for prey. A cheetah has extremely keen eyesight and can spot a herd of gazelles far away.

Sometimes a cheetah hunts by stalking its prey, but often it does not bother to conceal itself. A cheetah relies on speed rather than surprise to conquer its prey. The gazelles watch the cheetah approach, but wait until it is a serious threat before fleeing. When the cheetah is within a few hundred yards of them, they run. The cheetah then selects one of the animals as its victim and pursues it.

Thompson's gazelle.

Springing forward on powerful legs, a hunting cheetah races across the African plain. Over short distances, no other animal can run as fast as the cheetah. From a dead stop a cheetah can accelerate to 43 miles (69.4 kilometers) an hour in two seconds, and in short bursts cheetahs have been known to reach speeds of 75 miles (121 kilometers) an hour.

Every part of the cheetah's body helps it to run fast. Keeping its head steady, the cheetah fixes its sight on the prey. As its long legs reach out,

sturdy claws grip the ground. Both the claws and pads on the bottom of its feet keep the feet from sliding and help the cheetah to change direction quickly. As the cheetah reaches full speed, its backbone bends and then extends, acting like a spring to propel the cheetah forward. Scientists think that the cheetah's long tail, which it holds straight out behind it, helps the animal to keep its balance when running.

The dewclaw is about 4 inches (10.3 centimeters) above the inside claw of the foot.

Even though other animals may cross the cheetah's path, it follows only one. A gazelle is fast and can dodge expertly, but a cheetah is also extremely agile and can change its direction to match. As the cheetah reaches the gazelle's side, it uses its paw to knock the other animal down. The sharp dewclaw, which is located on the inside of each foreleg, hooks the victim and helps to pull it over.

Then the cheetah bites the animal in the throat to kill it.

After killing a large animal, the cheetah usually drags it to a shady spot. There the cheetah rests before beginning to eat its meal. Cheetahs tire easily and are often exhausted after making a kill. Although they can run fast in short bursts, cheetahs do not have much endurance over long distances.

34

In the wild, a cheetah mother needs to kill one animal a day to have enough food for herself and her cubs. A single animal usually hunts only every other day. To duplicate the wild cheetahs' eating cycle, the cheetahs at Wildlife Safari are given 3 to 5 pounds (1.4 to 2.3 kilograms) of meat for three days in a row. On the fourth day they are not fed. In addition to its regular diet, each cheetah is also fed a small piece of meat that has been coated with vitamins and minerals.

Meat coated with vitamins and minerals.

A cheetah has well-developed canine teeth, the long sharp teeth on each side of the mouth. These are ideally suited for piercing and tearing meat. In the back of the mouth, the cheetah has flatter teeth, called molars, which are used for grinding and cutting. Like other cats, a cheetah eats on the side of its mouth, pulling and tearing at raw chunks of meat.

Cheetahs get most of the water they need from their meat. Although they will go to a waterhole or river when they need to drink, they can go ten days or more without water. At Wildlife Safari, however, Damara has a bowl of water in her enclosure so she can drink whenever she gets thirsty.

Since cheetahs rely on sight for hunting, they are more active in the day than at night. In warm weather, they move around most during the early morning and late afternoon, when the temperatures are cooler. Even so, like most cats, cheetahs spend much of their time either asleep or at rest, getting up occasionally to stretch and change positions. Each of the cheetahs at Wildlife Safari seems to have its favorite place for napping. Usually they rest out in the open, although when it rains hard they find places in the shelters. In hot weather they sleep in the shade; when it is cold, they curl up into tight balls and their fur helps keep them warm. At Wildlife Safari the cheetahs live outdoors year round. Winters are mild near the Oregon coast and not much colder than the cool nights on the African plain.

Like other cats, cheetahs clean themselves regularly. A cheetah washes itself by licking its fur with its long, rough tongue to remove dirt, burrs, or loose fur. Occasionally two cheetahs lick each other. To deal with itches along its back, a cheetah either rubs against a tree or rolls on the ground.

Cheetahs in the wild do not live in specific territories that they defend, as many other animals do. But they do tend to space themselves out on the plain. This helps to ensure that there will be enough food for all, and provides a separate hunting area for each animal.

Most wild cheetahs live alone. However, sometimes two or more single males meet and form a small group called a *coalition*. The group may stay together for a few days or permanently. At the park, two brothers from the same litter have stayed together all their lives.

Wild cheetahs that hunt together tend to be healthier because they are more successful at killing prey and therefore get more food. Males in groups also tend to have more opportunities to breed.

A cheetah has a good sense of smell. If it enters a new area and smells recent markings of another cheetah, it will leave. A cheetah marks the area in which it is living by spraying urine on trees or rocks. The smell of the urine is a signal for other cheetahs to stay out.

Cheetahs are not aggressive animals and do not usually fight with each other unless they have to. The main cause is usually when two males fight over a female. Females do not fight with each other, although they will defend their cubs against predators.

If another animal threatens a cheetah, the cheetah will first growl and hiss at it. Then, if the animal continues to approach, the cheetah will lunge at it and stamp its front feet. Cheetahs also growl at other animals, such as leopards or hyenas, that try to steal their food.

Cheetahs are known to live as long as seventeen years. However, only some of these years are ones in which they can produce young. One of the most serious problems in trying to increase the number of cheetahs in the world is the fact that cheetahs are not able to produce enough cubs for the population to grow.

In most species, individual animals vary somewhat from each other—they have slightly different fur color, body size, or physical abilities. These differences are controlled in the body by tiny chemicals called genes. Normally, each individual has a unique set of genes that is different from anyone else's. Over time these differences in the genes allow some animals within a species to change and adapt to new circumstances.

Because there are so few cheetahs left in the world, they mate with only a limited number of other cheetahs. This inbreeding has created cheetahs whose genes are all nearly alike, so as with other purebred animals, cheetahs suffer from a lack of variety within the species. One of the problems with this is that it often produces weak animals or animals that are more likely to get sick. Thus fewer animals grow to be strong, healthy adults; and as a result not many babies are born.

When breeding animals in captivity, it is important to make sure that when they do mate, they are as distantly related as possible. People in zoos and wildlife parks now keep records of all their cheetahs, the cheetahs' parents, and their offspring. This information is used to coordinate breeding plans among various animal institutions. It is part of a larger program dedicated to learning more about cheetahs, and it is the only way that zoos and wildlife parks can continue to produce cheetahs for exhibit. This program is called the species survival plan (SSP). There are species survival plans for other endangered species as well.

It is difficult to say how much longer cheetahs will be able to survive in the wild. Even though laws protect the cheetah, it is often hard for governments to enforce them. In some places cheetahs are still killed for their fur or when farmers fear that the animals are eating their livestock. Perhaps the most serious danger to cheetahs, and to other animals of the African plain, is the shrinking of their homeland as more and more wild land is used for ranching and agriculture.

Most of us will never have the chance to see cheetahs in the wild, but by getting to know animals like Damara and observing cheetahs in zoos and wildlife parks, we can begin to appreciate the cheetah's unique and special qualities. Time is running out for the fastest animal on earth. It is important that we do everything we can to preserve its existence.

INDEX

Photographs are in **boldface.**